Donald Trump Candidacy According to Matthew?

Donald Trump Candidacy According to Matthew?

A Monograph Analyzing the Donald Trump Candidacy —A Biblical Non-Political Perspective

J. Bartholomew Walker

Quadrakoff Publications Group, LLC
Wilmington, Delaware
USA

Copyright © 2019, 2016 Quadrakoff Publications Group, LLC All rights reserved.

Except as noted, All NASB scriptures taken from The New American Standard Bible® Copyright © 1960, 1962, 1963, 1968, 1971, 1972, 1973, 1975, 1977, 1995 by the Lockman Foundation, LaHabra, CA.

Special thanks to the Lockman Foundation for the finest Bible version available; as well as for their permission to use the same. All Scripture passages taken from The Holy Bible, King James Version, are as noted.

ISBN: 978-1-948219-16-7

All rights reserved. No part of this publication may be reproduced, stored in a retrieval system or transmitted, in any form, or by any means, electronic, mechanical, recorded, photocopied, or otherwise, without the prior written permission of both the copyright owner and the above publisher of this book, except by a reviewer who may quote brief passages in a review.

The scanning, uploading, and distribution of this book via the Internet or via any other means without the permission of the publisher is illegal and punishable by law. Please purchase only authorized electronic editions and do not participate in or encourage electronic piracy of copyrightable materials. Your support of the author's rights is appreciated.

Any and all characters appearing that are not in any of the versions of the Bible are fictional. Any resemblance to any living person is strictly coincidental.

Printed in the United States of America.

FOREWORD

Unbeknownst to me, JB and Emma had been watching something develop before their eyes, and had made some interesting observations.

So JB comes to me and tells me that he wants to publish a monograph about the Trump candidacy. He was working on an upcoming publication, and believed that some of his research might very well apply to the Trump candidacy. As Bible based publishers, this presented a bit of a problem; as we generally stay away from politics. It is true that some believe "*Statists Saving One*" represents a politically leaning work, but this is actually not so. "*Statists*" is largely about the enemy's machinations, with any political leader's involvement being only secondary. In fact, at times we have heard similar comments with regard to "*Statists*" being anti-religion. These are only correct, insofar as there is involvement and commonality with the actions and objectives of the enemy.

The purpose of "Donald Trump Candidacy According to Matthew?" was to analyze the *process*, and not to in any way endorse any political ideology or candidate. Quite predictably there were those who claimed that this was precisely what we did, but none could cite any evidence of this.

It is important to understand the timeframe in which this work was written. April of 2016, was about ten months after Donald Trump had announced his candidacy. The establishment Republicans resented Trumps entry, and some were willing to do almost anything to stop him. After all, Trump was not "next in line," and those who believed that it was they who in fact were; simply hated him. This had little to do with political ideology, but rather the maintaining of the establishment, also referred to as "the swamp"—which is largely about power, irrespective of political leanings.

If what was believed to be so was in fact so, then the chances of Donald Trump losing the presidential election were next to nothing. It mattered not what the polls said at any given time. If this were all true, then Trump was going to win, as no other outcome was possible.

We (at QPG) individually watched the election returns, with the tacit knowledge that somehow Trump would prevail. This was not in any way related to any personal views about Donald Trump, as these are private matters. Rather, we believed that we were witnessing in "real time" precisely that which Jesus had taught. To the extent that one believed this was so; to that very same extent one was certain of Trump's victory—irrespective of one's political views.

Finally; now several years after the publication of this monograph; there is one other "test" as to whether or

Foreword

not the process analyzed in this monograph was in fact the means by which Donald Trump became president—this of course being the post-victory *behavior* of his political opponents. Specifically; have Trump's political opponents been behaving in a manner consistent with their purported "moral and ethical" principles? Or did the "push" created by Donald Trump's victory reveal "that which actually is?"

Malcolm F. Sutton,
Editor in Chief
QPG, LLC

> *Dunamis or supernatural power, and dynamikós or natural power, are separate and distinct entities. When any power disobeys natural law; by definition this has to be dunamis—if it is in fact the case that natural law is violated. Whether this power is to one's liking or not changes nothing with respect to what it is. But dunamis or supernatural power rarely, if ever, occurs as a single unit.*

Donald Trump Candidacy According to Matthew?

Back in June of 2015, Emma and I were watching the news, and analyzing the announcement of Donald Trump seeking the presidency of the United States.

It took a while to observe all of the factors, but we were quite aware of what Yogi Berra is reputed to have said: "You can observe a lot by watching." So we watched, and watched, and still watched.

We especially watched the "experts," hearing the word "apoplectic" so many times, that I was forced to look it up to make sure it was being utilized correctly—and it seems that most of the time it was.

Finally I looked at Emma and said: "I think he (Donald Trump) might have a talantŏn." Emma kind of looked at me for a while and then said: "I think you may be correct. There really is no other possible explanation."

April 2016,
Wilmington, DE

Now precisely what is a talantŏn? It cannot be looked up in an English dictionary, as it is not a word in English. The best one generally can do is to find an explanation related to the Bible that is often quite misleading, and quite incorrect.

Talantŏn is often considered to be the root of the word *talent*. Talent as used in the Biblical sense is generally considered to be a Hebrew unit of weight; with there often being differences between a *common* talent and a *royal* talent. However the root of talent is the Greek word *talantŏn*, and is not a Hebrew word. Thus this relationship to a unit of *physical* weight was inserted later, with *talent* proffered as a Hebrew word; which it is not, and never was.

Donald Trump Candidacy According to Matthew?

But it cannot be overemphasized that a talent or talantŏn is not a mere unit of weight such as an ounce, a pound, a ton or a kilogram. These are mere *objective* units of measure for the "*quantity* of a thing." A talent or talantŏn is much less objective and much less quantifiable than this. A talent or talantŏn is a *subjective* weight that is a balancing weight, or a weight to be carried.

A talent or talantŏn is thus a balancing weight for something else; but whether or not it is ultimately actually *carried* is a matter of one's choice. That "something else" or *balance* for a talantŏn is known as *dunamis*; and in the New Testament dunamis is used to indicate and is properly translated as "*supernatural* power." This is in comparison to the Greek word *dynamikós*, which is *natural* power.

There is a Hebrew word which indicates the presence of *both* this supernatural power (Greek *dunamis*), *and* this weight (Greek *talantŏn*); and this Hebrew word is *massâ'*. It is for this reason that *massâ'* is sometimes translated with words such as "oracle;" and is sometimes translated as some type of "weight" in the Old Testament.

Having recently reviewed a Chapter about this very same subject for an upcoming new book, (currently in post production); we thought it appropriate to release some excerpts from that Chapter at this time. These excerpts have been abridged so as to only include details we believe provide the necessary background which is pertinent to understanding the subject of this monograph.

To be clear, this is not in any way any type of

political *endorsement* of anyone; but rather to merely provide a Biblical explanation for a phenomenon that up to this point has been inexplicable. It must also be noted that because of time constraints, this is the "beta" version.

In the interest of accuracy, the diacritics for these words were included in this introduction, and are necessarily maintained in the following chapter excerpts:

Beginning of excerpt:

[. . . In Matthew 25:14-30 we are told the famous parable of the talents. We know that this is a parable and not an actual story, because generally when Jesus told parables, no proper names were used. When it is a recollection of actual events, usually proper names were used.

It must be noted that in Luke 19:12-27 there exists a similar story. These two parables can easily be conflated, but there are very significant differences between them. Because of these differences, it seems unlikely that Matthew and Luke are merely have differing accounts of the same event; but rather that only one account is correct—that of course being the one that makes the most sense.

In order to maintain intellectual honesty, this parable is first presented here in its entirety

Following is Matthew 25:14-30, with the verse numbers removed for ease of reading:

"For it is just like a man

Donald Trump Candidacy According to Matthew?

*about to go on a journey,
who called his own slaves
and entrusted his possessions to them.
To one he gave five talents,
to another, two, and to another,
one, each according to his own ability;
and he went on his journey.*

*Immediately the one who had received the
five talents went and traded with them,
and gained five more talents.
In the same manner the one who had
received the two talents gained two more.
But he who received the one talent went
away, and dug a hole in the ground
and hid his master's money.*

*Now after a long time the master of those
slaves came and settled accounts with
them.*

*The one who had received the five talents
came up and brought five more talents,
saying, 'Master, you entrusted five talents
to me. See, I have gained five more
talents.' His master said to him,
'Well done, good and faithful slave.
You were faithful with a few things,
I will put you in charge of many things;
enter into the joy of your master.'*

*Also the one who had received the two
talents came up and said, 'Master, you
entrusted two talents to me. See, I have*

J. Bartholomew Walker

gained two more talents. 'His master said to him, 'Well done, good and faithful slave.

You were faithful with a few things, I will put you in charge of many things; enter into the joy of your master.'

And the one also who had received the one talent came up and said, 'Master, I knew you to be a hard man, reaping where you did not sow and gathering where you scattered no seed. 'And I was afraid, and went away and hid your talent in the ground. See, you have what is yours.'

But his master answered and said to him, 'You wicked, lazy slave, you knew that I reap where I did not sow and gather where I scattered no seed. 'Then you ought to have put my money in the bank, and on my arrival I would have received my money back with interest. Therefore take away the talent from him, and give it to the one who has the ten talents.'

For to everyone who has, more shall be given, and he will have an abundance; but from the one who does not have, even what he does have shall be taken away. Throw out the worthless slave into the outer darkness; in that place there will

Donald Trump Candidacy According to Matthew?

be weeping and gnashing of teeth.'

The way it reads, this slave master decides to go on a journey. So before he leaves, he calls his three slaves in for a meeting, and distributes all of his possessions to these three. It doesn't actually say all, but that is a fair read. He gives them these talents according to their ability. Likely the *head* slave got five, the *middle* slave two, and the *apprentice* slave one.

He then gives no instructions whatsoever as to what should be done with these possessions. Neither does he indicate if or when he will be returning; nor is there any indication as to *if* or *when* what he "*gave*" the "slaves;" it does state "gave;" is to be returned to him.

He finally comes back. In his absence, two of the slaves traded the talents and resulting in 100% profit. One slave hid the talent by burying it in the ground. It is not actually stated whether any or all of these slaves individually had the title of "the apprentice."

So what does the slave master then do? He congratulates the two who risked his money by trading, and allows them both to keep not only all of the original money, but also lets them keep their profits as well. But to the one who hid the money; a rather conservative investment guaranteeing principal; he rebukes him, takes the money back and gives it to the one who now has ten, making it eleven for one servant, and zero for the other.

What principle are we to learn from this parable? *"For to everyone who has, more shall be given, and he will have an abundance; but from the one who does not have, even what he does have shall be taken away."*

So then by this reasoning; in life, the appropriate *Christian* thing to do would then be to find the "least of these" and take away some of what they already have. Since this clearly would contradict many of Jesus' other teachings, this simply cannot be the point of this story.

In order to understand the wisdom contained in this parable, the logical very first question to be asked is precisely what was it that Jesus was actually speaking *about*? Part of this answer is contained in the very first sentence, wherein it states: "For *it* is just like..." (emphasis added)   The question then becomes: "Precisely what is it that "it" represents; that is "*just like*" that which follows?"

"It" is a third person pronoun, referring to something else.   "It" represents a rather large category of actualities. In fact, anything not being masculine or feminine in nature would qualify to be included in this "it" category.

To find the meaning of this particular "it," going all the way back to the beginning of the chapter where this story later appears; Matthew 25:1; provides some insight.

Matthew Chapter 25 begins with 25:1, where Jesus is speaking and tells us:

> *"Then the kingdom of heaven will be comparable to..."*[12]

Thus it seems likely that Jesus is also speaking about this very same "kingdom of heaven," in this parable which is also contained in Chapter 25, but in later verses 14-30—in some way or manner.

However, it must be noted that here in verse 1, Jesus is speaking about what *"will be;"* whereas later in verse 14, (where this "Talent Man" story begins), He is speaking about what currently *"is:" "For it is just like a man..."*

Jesus indicated in verse 1 what the Kingdom of Heaven *"will be;"* and will be *"then,"* or at some *future* time, as the verse begins with *"then."* Therefore this *"will be"* cannot be now, or at least was not yet at the time Jesus said this. This is an important distinction, because what the *"kingdom of heaven"* currently *"is"*, is something which affects our lives *now*; as opposed to what it *"will be,"* at whatever time the *"then"* represents; which *will not* affect us, at least not directly, until the *"then."*

Precisely what is this "kingdom of heaven?" Generally, there are two definitions of "heaven," depending on whether the singular or the plural is used; and whether or not preceded by the definite article: "the."

Heaven in the singular is generally understood to be where God resides, and a place where our immortal "pneuma," or *soul*, begins its journey; and with salvation, the place to where it will ultimately return.

It is never, (except by Petrovsky), referred to as "the heaven."

"*The heavens*" however, generally refers to the sky and outward. "Heavens" is generally referred to in the plural and rarely without the "the." The "s" in the phrase: "For heaven's sake," is possessive and not plural.

It is interesting to again inquire as to precisely where God was when he created the heavens and the earth. Clearly he was not yet residing in a place that had yet to be created. Thus, as previously addressed, clearly there must be two different meanings for this word "heaven."

The actual Greek word in Matthew 25:1 which is translated as "heaven" is:

> "3772 ŏuranŏs; perh.from the same as 3735 (through the idea of *elevation*); the *sky*; by extens. *heaven* (as the abode of God); by impl. *happiness, power, eternity*; spec. the *Gospel, (Christianity)*: - air, heaven ([-ly]), sky."[3]

> "3735 ŏrŏs; prob. from an obsol. ŏrō (to *rise* or "*rear*"; perh. akin to *142*; comp. *3733*); a *mountain* (as *lifting* itself above the plain): - hill, mount (-ain)."[4]

In Luke 11:2; where the "Lord's prayer" appears; (≈Our Father who art in heaven. . .); "heaven" is also 3772 ŏuranŏs.[5]

If a fair analysis of this word "heaven" or ŏuranŏs is undertaken, it would initially seem that the meaning has much more to do with physical elevation, air, to rise or to rear, lifting, a hill, or a mountain, rather than the abode of God; which according to Strong's, is derived only by extension of ŏuranŏs.

However; from Jesus Himself using an Aramaic word which translates to the Greek word ŏuranŏs; both in Luke when providing the "Lord's Prayer;" and here in Matthew, at the beginning of Chapter 25; it seems clear that He is speaking of "Heaven" where the Father is, and not "the heavens," where celestial bodies revolve. Furthermore; this parable in no way resembles any type of Astronomy lecture. One might try to argue that the "Master" represents the Sun, and the three servants the three innermost planets or some such; but this would likely be highly unsuccessful—unless some type of hallucinogens were also involved.

The actual word translated as "kingdom" is:

> "932 basilĕia; from 935; prop. *royalty*, i.e. (abstr.) *rule*, or (concr.) a *realm* (lit. or fig.): - kingdom + reign."[6]

So it would seem reasonable to conclude that the "it" to which Jesus is referring with respect to the parable, is the "kingdom of heaven." And this likely refers not only to the "place" in which God resides; but rather, refers to the entire *immaterial* realm, and the rules associated therein.

"In verse 1 of Matthew 25, Jesus referred to what the kingdom of heaven "*will be*" at the "*then*." Here in this parable, in verse 14 of Matthew 25, He is speaking of what heaven *is*, and *is now*.

The parable was spoken by Jesus in Aramaic, and written in Greek. Thus there are only inexact synonyms for terminology between Greek and the Old Testament Hebrew equivalents; and that is only part of the problem.

Jesus told us: *"For it is just like a man about to go on a journey, who called his own slaves and entrusted his possessions to them. To one he gave five talents, to another, two, and to another, one, each according to his own ability; and he went on his journey."*

According to Strong's, the word *slave* (singular) actually appears only once in the entire Bible; in Jeremiah 2:14, where a distinction is being made between a slave and a servant.[7]

And the word *slaves* (plural), only appears once in the entire Bible, and is in Revelation 18:13. And in Revelation, the actual word translated as "slaves" is *soma*, generally meaning body.[8]

The actual Greek word translated as "slaves" here in Matthew is:

> "*1401* dŏulŏs; from *1210*; a slave (lit. or fig., invol or vol.; frequently therefore in a qualified sense of subjection or subserviency): - bond (-man), servant."[9]

This may seem a bit crazy; in that Strong's does not list *slave* (singular) as appearing anywhere in the entire Bible, except in Jeremiah; and yet the very first word in the definition of dŏulŏs is slave. It gets a bit worse, as

Strong provides *nothing* for the actual word in Jeremiah that is translated as slave (singular).[10]

Thus it is a fair conclusion, at least according to Strong, that there is no original word known in the entire Bible that corresponds to slave in the singular; and only a word meaning *body* that is translates as slaves in the plural; the first word in the definition of dŏulŏs notwithstanding. In fact, Strongest Strong's classifies the word "slave" as "NIH" meaning "Not in Hebrew," citing Jeremiah as the example of an *added* word.[11]

Based upon the word dŏulŏs appearing elsewhere in the Bible, and always being translated as *servant* every other time; it seems likely that *slave* would be an incorrect translation. (This of course relates to the New Testament Greek.) Furthermore; according to Strong, dŏulŏs can be voluntary or involuntary, and thus could be either. Dŏulŏs appears to have to do with the *condition* of subservience or submission, rather than any specific type of *relationship* that produced this condition.

It is unclear precisely what it is that constitutes "voluntary slavery." Thus, *servant* seems to be the better definition for dŏulŏs—particularly in the context of the parable. In this parable, Jesus is explaining a mechanism by which God's servants (H. Sapiens) voluntarily; i.e.; free will choosing; to serve him.

The mistranslated word "talent" has several

definitions. It is sometimes a unit of weight which can range from 75 pounds for a *common* talent, to 150 pounds for a *royal* talent.[12]

In the entire Old Testament, the Hebrew word *translated* as "talent," except once, is:

> "3603 kikkâr; from 3769; a *circle*, i.e. (by impl.) a circumjacent *tract* or region, espec. the *Ghôr* or valley of the Jordan; also a (round) *loaf*; also a *talent* (or large [round] coin): - loaf, morsel, piece, plain, talent."[13]

This only other actual word translated as "talent' is:

> "3604 kikkêr (Chald.); corresp. to 3603; a *talent*; - talent."[14]

Thus the idea that "talent" is any type of Hebrew unit of measure; whether common or royal; is in no way supported factually. For whatever reason(s), translators elected to insert the word "talent" for *kikkâr* and *kikkêr* in the *Old Testament* translations.

The actual *Greek* word appearing in Matthew 25 translated as talent is:

> "5007 talantŏn; neut. Of a presumed der. of the orig. form of tiaō (to *bear*; equiv. to 5342); a *balance* (as *supporting* weights), i.e. (by impl.) a certain *weight* (and thence a *coin* or rather *sum* of money) or "*talent*": - talent."[15]

Donald Trump Candidacy According to Matthew?

Here the concept of talent representing a certain weight is only by *implication*. This "implication" explanation is likely the "tail wagging the dog;" as Strong did his work in the late 19th century, long after many of the mistranslations by the "experts" had taken place.

The above stated "equivalent" word for talantŏn is:

"5342 phĕrō; a prim. verb...to *"bear"* or *carry*"[16]

And of course, there is the common definition of talent; which refers to capabilities, generally considered to be innate; allowing someone to be able to, or have the capability to perform certain things in a manner which far exceeds the norm. *Talent* refers to this capability, *talented* refers to the individual who has the talent, and *gifted* is a term often used to describe the process whereby, or the reason the talented individual received or has said talent; and and as will be seen, this; (gifted); is more than arguably a misnomer.

There is a distinct difference between the meanings of the Old Testament Hebrew *kikkâr* or *kikkêr*; irrespective of its incorrect translation as talent; and the New Testament Greek *talantŏn*. The Hebrew essentially means circle, the meaning related to money likely only from the shape of a coin. [*There exists a derogatory word for Jewish people which will not be repeated here. Many believe that the root of this word is kikkâr. The reason likely has to do with illiterate Jewish immigrants to the United States having to sign their name and refusing to sign with an "X," because of the similarities to the Christian cross; thus instead signing their name with a circle.*]

The Greek word *talantŏn* has nothing whatsoever to do with any shape; including the circle. Rather, it represents bearing, balance and perhaps; but only by implication; a specified and accurate weight. A twenty dollar US gold coin is just shy of one ounce troy pure gold. It is circular, but also represents a specific certain weight of gold. *Kikkâr* could be used to describe this as a coin, or its value as a coin, and some small fraction of the weight of the Hebrew "phantom" talent could *incorrectly* be used to describe its weight in gold. The confusion between the meanings of the terms may have arisen from this relationship.

However, the original Greek word used in the parable is *talantŏn*. Thus it would be prudent to assume that the *actual* definition of the *actual* word *actually* used, is what Jesus *actually* meant. Therefore, it would be fair to say that each of the servants was given a weight to bear, a weight or something as a balance to something else, and from the *immaterial* perspective a "certain" weight. The use of "certain weight" can be interpreted two ways. It can refer to the *amount* of the weight as certain, such as one ounce troy; or it can refer to the *existence* of some *balancing* weight as a certainty; irrespective of the amount.

Since the definitions of *talantŏn* primarily have to do with the act of bearing, carrying, balancing etc., irrespective of the *amount* of any weight, this appears to be the correct meaning; rather than a sum of money or weight of precious metals equivalent to some agreed upon value. The use of *talantŏn* as money, is never literal, but only by implication. How much *talantŏn* was each given and why? They were each given different amounts based upon their abilities. It must be noted that they were not each given *talantŏn* according to their *accomplishments*, but rather according to their *abilities*—not according to what they had *done*, but rather according to what they were *capable* of doing.

The actual Greek word translated here as "ability" is the aforementioned:

> "*1411* dunamis; from *1410*; *force* (lit. or fig.); spec. miraculous *power* (usually by impl. a *miracle* itself): - ability, abundance, meaning, might (-ily, -y, -y deed), worker of) miracle (-s), power, strength, violence, mighty (wonderful) work."[17]

This word *dunamis*; must clearly be distinguished from the English word "dynamic;" which is derived from the Greek word *dynamikós*, which means "powerful; dýnamis, which means power; and dýnasthai, which means be able or have power."[18]

The abilities referenced in this parable were their *supernatural* or *miraculous* abilities (dunamis); and not any type of *natural* abilities (dynamikós). This is not to say that they did not have any natural abilities; but rather that their natural abilities are not referenced, and thus have nothing to do with the parable.

In physics, the derived word *dyne* represents a measurement or unit of *natural* force existing in the *material* realm; which when applied to a *mass*, results in *work* or the movement of the mass.

There seems to yet be no equivalent word derived from *dunamis*; which would represent a measurement or unit of *supernatural* force in the *immaterial* realm; which when applied, results in work or the movement of possibly immaterial phenomenon, or more relevant to this parable; capable of ultimately making resultant changes in *material* phenomenon; but here from *dunamic* (supernatural) and not *dynamic* (natural) factors.

This being the case: the word *duna* is hereby coined, and is defined as the unit of measure of immaterial force, capable of making material changes *via* the *immaterial* realm. It must be pointed out that although the force acts in the *immaterial* realm, the ultimate purpose is to affect changes in the *material* realm; and thus does not exclusively result in changes solely in the immaterial realm.

Although an exact accepted value, quantity or magnitude of a *duna* cannot actually be numerically calculated at this time, it can nevertheless be used to measure *relative* amounts of supernatural power. If this seems idiotic, absurd or useless; it must be remembered that in mathematics, "i" represents a quantity equaling the value of the square root of negative one. With respect to "i," this represents an *imaginary* number; as there is no known number when multiplied by itself will yield a negative product; hence the choice of that particular letter for the variable. The square root of a negative number simply does not exist; or at least has no actuality in our material world. But with respect to *duna*, immaterial power does exist.

Thus unlike in mathematics; where a term was selected to quantify a non-existent entity; here it is a bit different, in that it is the *quantification* of the something which *does* exist into a unit, albeit that only the *relative* value, and not the *actual* value is known.

Again, the key to this definition of *dunamis* is that it is *supernatural* or "miraculous," or a "miracle," or "wonderful," (full of wonder), force or power. This is not merely *natural* or *dynamikós* power or ability, but rather a *supernatural* or *miraculous* type of power.

Thus, each "servant" was given a *talantŏn* or weight to bear or balance or support; arguably of denoted measurable value, according to the amount of *dunamis* or supernatural power each had. There is a relationship between the terms. Because of the amount of *dunamis* or supernatural power given or possessed, there is a corresponding balancing weight or *responsibility* or *talantŏn*.

In order to avoid confusion, it would be prudent at this juncture to assign a term to describe and relatively quantify this amount of weight to bear or responsibility (*talantŏn*). This is necessary as said *talantŏn*, in this usage does not refer to *objective* physical weight as could be measured on a physical scale, but rather the *subjective* weight to the host.

This being the case: the word *tala* is hereby coined, and is defined as a unit of measure of immaterial, subjective, psychological, or emotional weight, capable of causing the host to exercise; and arguably is required to balance; his or her level of *dunamis*. The term *tala* must be used to avoid confusion with the *erroneous* translation as *talent* as a unit of *physical* weight, (pound, ounce, etc); or talent as innate *skill* which is completely free; i.e.; "gifted."

One could hypothetically assign a value of one *duna* per *tala*. Thus the servant who received five *tala*, was given this "weight" of five *tala*, because he had five *duna* of supernatural power. Likewise, the same could be said for the two, and one "talent" servants.

The failure to realize this, would likely result in a classic example of the failure to perceive sufficient actuality; or perhaps better phrased; a failure to sufficiently perceive *the* actuality. Given that this may seem somewhat tautological or oxymoronic; this includes: to fail to perceive even in a somewhat limited sense; the; or an; actuality *in-toto*.

The presence of *dunamis* or supernatural power is often incorrectly perceived and is generally considered to be a stand alone entity—meaning that the *dunamis* alone represents the entire actuality. But in fact, it is *both* the *dunamis* or supernatural power; *and* the *talantŏn* or the balancing weight or responsibility; that comprises the true one actuality. They each individually represent only a part of the actuality. This is why using the term "gifted" would be inaccurate; as "gifted" recognizes only the *dunamis*; and not the associated and inextricably linked *talantŏn*.

Donald Trump Candidacy According to Matthew?

Proverbs 30:1 begins with the following:

> *"The words of Agur the son of Jakeh, the oracle."*[9]

The King James translation is: "even the prophesy," in place of "the oracle."[20]

And Malachi 1:1 begins with the following:

> *"The oracle of the word of the LORD to Israel through Malachi."*[21]

In both of these verses, the word "oracle" appears. A fair interpretation of an oracle; is one who is able to provide revelation. Whether providing prophesy or retrophesy, oracles clearly exercise *dunamis*; at least when acting in the capacity of an oracle.

However; the *King James* translation of this very same Malachi 1:1, provides "burden" as the translation, rather than "oracle:"

The KJV of Malachi 1:1 is:

> *"The burden of the word of the LORD to Israel by Malachi."*[22]

The actual word translated as "oracle" in both verses is:

> "4853 massâ'; from 5375; a *burden*; spec. *tribute*, or (abstr.) *porterage*; fig. an *utterance*,..." chiefly a *doom*, espec. *singing*; mental, *desire*: - burden, carry away, prophesy, x they set, song, tribute."[23]

> "5375 nâsâ' or nâcâh; a prim. root; to *lift* in a great variety of applications.[24]

"Porterage" generally refers to carrying a weight or burden; e.g.; a porter.

Thus there are several seemingly unrelated meanings to massâ' et seq. They can be translated as an *utterance*, likely prophetic or retrophesitic in nature; as well as a *burden* or *lifting*; as well as *desire* and *ability*.

As a result, it seems clear that massâ' represents the understanding or comprehension of a given actuality in Hebrew; for which the use of both *dunamis* as well as *talantŏn*, and comprehending their relationship; is required for understanding or comprehending of the very same actuality in Greek—[(Hebrew) *massâ'* = (Greek) *dunamis* + (Greek) *talantŏn*].

Dunamis may *appear* to exist alone; but cannot exist without the corresponding talantŏn. However; the mere *existence* of the talantŏn, does not necessarily mean it will be carried.

Luke 12:48 confirms this spiritual or immaterial rule of balance by telling us:

Donald Trump Candidacy According to Matthew?

> *"...From everyone who has
> been given much,
> much will be required;
> and to whom they entrusted much,
> of him they will ask all the more."*[25]

Here in Luke, the aforementioned concept of the Hebrew word massâ'; or the requirement that among other things; the quantity of both *"dunamis + talantŏn"* necessarily be considered in order to ascertain an actuality, is confirmed.

And Jesus goes on with the parable: *"Immediately the one who had received the five talents went and traded with them, and gained five more talents. In the same manner the one who had received the two talents gained two more. But he who received the one talent went away, and dug a hole in the ground and hid his master's money."*

A cursory reading seems pretty simple. Two of the men took the money and traded with it, resulting in a profit of 100%—except for two minor problems. The same being: that it *(talantŏn)* was not money, but that burden which is necessarily associated with supernatural power; and it is not precisely known what is actually meant by "traded."

The original Greek word translated as "traded" is:

> "*2038* ĕrgazŏmai; mid. from *2041*; to *toil* (as a task, occupation, etc.)..."[26]

> "2041 ĕrgŏn; from a prim. (but obsol.) ĕrgō (to work); *toil* (as an effort or occupation); by impl. and act: - deed, doing, labour, work."[27]

Ĕrgazŏmai is the root of the term ergs, energy, and ergonomics.

The term "traded" can be misleading, as it can refer to a situation where possession of items can be exchanged or swapped, without any corresponding increase in total wealth. "Trading" may result in increase in wealth for the parties involved in the exchange, but there is no increase in *total* societal wealth. There is no actual work being done in the literal sense, so there is no increase in total wealth.

Clearly the definition of ĕrgazŏmai requires actual "work," "toil," effort, etc., and thus can refer to "trades" such as the construction *trade*; which *can* increase total wealth, because the value or amount of wealth in the final product exceeds the value or wealth of the components.

Precisely what type of work or *ĕrgazŏmai* was it in which these servants engaged? It appears from the definition of *dunamis*, that it likely was miraculous work; "spec.(ifically) miraculous power (usually by impl. a miracle itself)."

Here they worked their *dunamis*; or supernatural power, and not any *dynamikós*; or natural power.

Proverbs 14:23 tells us:

"In all labor there is profit,

Donald Trump Candidacy According to Matthew?

But mere talk leads only to poverty."[28]

The parable continues:
"*Now after a long time the master of those slaves came and settled accounts with them.*

"*The one who had received the five talents came up and brought five more talents, saying, 'Master, you entrusted five talents to me. See, I have gained five more talents.'* "*His master said to him, 'Well done, good and faithful slave. You were faithful with a few things, I will put you in charge of many things; enter into the joy of your master.'*

"*Also the one who had received the two talents came up and said, 'Master, you entrusted two talents to me. See, I have gained two more talents.'* "*His master said to him, 'Well done, good and faithful slave. You were faithful with a few things, I will put you in charge of many things; enter into the joy of your master.*"

What seems to be happening here; is that these two servants went out and "worked" their supernatural or miraculous abilities, far beyond what was required by the magnitude of their responsibilities. They began by being given a quantity of *tala* or weight to bear, according to the number of *duna* they each had possessed; as that is essentially what is stated. If the hypothetical relationship holds; one was given 5 tala, because he had 5 duna. The other was given 2 tala, because he had 2 duna. But they fulfilled their responsibilities so well, that they were ultimately given more tala. But the *actuality* includes both tala and duna. Meaning; that one cannot have one without the other.

And the "master's" response was consistent with this. They were put "*in charge of many things*."

The "*in charge of*" is actually:

> "2525 kathistēmi; from 2596 and 2476; to *place down* (permanently), i.e. (fig.) to *designate, constitute, convoy*: - appoint, be, conduct, make ordain, set."[29]

The word "things" does not appear in the original Greek. There exists no word which could be translated as "things" in this passage. The word "things" appears to have been added at some point in time, for whatever purported reason(s). This later addition of "things" results not in clarity, but confusion and obfuscation; by opening up tremendous and arguably unlimited possibilities as to what these "things" actually were. This is not quite as bad as the tendency today to call anything and everything immaterial "spirit," but nevertheless results in substantial confusion. The few and the many are correct; but no other word or words appear in this section regarding to what the few and many refer.

Thus, there is no explanation whatsoever provided as to the nature of the additional "things" they were put in charge of. Neither is there any detailed explanation of the original "few" with which they were "faithful;" except as stated in the beginning of the parable.

This being that the *few* and *many* were related to either these supernatural or miraculous powers, or *dunamis*; or they were related to the *talantŏn*; or to

Donald Trump Candidacy According to Matthew?

"bear or balance as supporting weights." Since they had already received the additional talantŏn or units of talas as a result of their work or "ergs; then by Hobson's choice, both the "few" and the "many" must refer to the units of duna.

It being the case that the few things with which they were faithful represented these miraculous powers; and it being the case that no additional description is provided about the additional "many" over which they were given *kathistēmi*, but only that there is some relationship between what was done with the "few" as a causative factor resulting in the statement about the "many."

Had there been a difference between the types of things that the few represented, and the subsequent many things, then likely this would have been stated. Thus, unlike it being possible by the later addition of "things;" it is not the character, characteristics or nature of the additional things over which they were given charge that is being stated, but rather solely concerning the *number* or *amount* of something.

This of course makes perfect sense, as the additional units of tala, or balancing weight taken on by them, had to be counterbalanced by obtaining additional units of duna.

The alternative explanation being; that the "few" and the "many" simply refer to the amount of *money* originally given to each of them; this arguably being like being given charge over few and many dollars. Aside from the previously mentioned problems associated with this position, there are more:

Firstly, if the position is taken that the above is

all gibberish, and talent is merely a unit of *normal* weight; then likely between 375 and 750 pounds of weight was originally given to the *five* talent man; as it does not state whether these "talents" were *common* or *royal*.

Thus, when he returned, he would have been carrying between 750 and 1,500 pounds of weight. Along with this, is the problem that unless it is known what *material* it was of which the five talent man was originally carrying 375-750 pounds, there is no way to determine the value, if any; of either the original five, or subsequent five.

Second, is the use of the word "few." This term *few* is usually reserved for a quantity of more than two; as two is generally referred to as a *couple*; yet he stated the very same thing to the two talent man. Thus, it seems more than just speculation to suggest that he would have said the same thing to the one talent man, had he been "faithful" with that one talent.

Third, there is the "faithful" issue. There is no mention of what it was these servants were either instructed or expected to do with these talents. Yet upon their return, there actions are described as faithful. This implies prior knowledge on the part of the servants with respect to this.

Fourthly, would or does the amount of money, rather than "money" itself qualify numerically for these statements about few and many? If so then the five talent man was given a *large* few, the two talent a *medium* few, and the one talent man arguably a *small* few. Or does it make more sense that the few and the many refer to either the numbers of dunas or to the number of sub-types of *dunamis* or supernatural/miraculous power?

If this part of the parable were told in English today, it would begin as: "The rule of the immaterial realm is like a man who called his persons of subservience and entrusted his possessions to him. To one he gave five tala of balancing weight, to another two tala and another one tala. This was done to each according to said servant's supernatural power, or ability to do miraculous things."

The following rules provide some keys to the understanding the interplay of natural and supernatural forces:

> I. "Nature will not permit the continued existence of an unbalanced actuality."

> II. "The universe will obey your will to the extent that it is not inconsistent with; nor contradictory to; the will of God."

> III. "When perceiving an *actuality*, one must exercise caution as to perceive as much of the actuality as possible, as this will determine one's *reality*; and it is our reality upon which we base our thoughts and actions. Likewise, caution must be exercised in order to not perceive as one actuality, that which is or are aspects of two separate actualities; or the reverse."

And the parable is concluded in two distinct parts: First part:

> "*And the one also who had received the one talent came up and said, 'Master, I knew you to be a hard man, reaping where you did not sow and gathering where you scattered no seed. 'And I was afraid, and went away and hid your talent in the ground. See, you have what is yours.'*"

Here in the first part, the servant is making three distinct statements:

1. He is calling the master a hard (not meek) hearted thief; as what other word better describes one who *reaps* where he did not sow and *gathering* where he had scattered no seed?
2. Secondly, he is stating that he was afraid of something, and because of this fear hid the talent in the ground.
3. Thirdly, the servant then seems to be trying to placate the master; by telling him that he now has something that belongs to the master; after just accusing him of whatever was his, (the master's); wasn't legitimately his, (the master's); in the first place.

Donald Trump Candidacy According to Matthew?

Second part:

> *"But his master answered and said to him, 'you wicked, lazy slave, you knew that I reap where I did not sow and gather where I scattered no seed. Then you ought to have put my money in the bank, and on my arrival I would have received my money back with interest. Therefore take away the talent from him, and give it to the one who has the ten talents." For to everyone who has, more shall be given, and he will have an abundance; but from the one who does not have, even what he does have shall be taken away."*

There are cause-effect relationships implied in this portion. This is so because of the appearance of the words "then" and "therefore"

What is actually being said by the master is: "*if*" what you (servant) are saying is true, "*then*" you ought to have. . ." Or more contemporarily phrased: "You knew that I was a thief huh? Then you should have. . ."

The talent being referred to as *money* in the story only happens two times: previously in Matthew 25:18, (appearing once: *"hid his master's money"*); when this servant's actions were described as if by a "third party" narration. And then again (appearing twice here: *"Then you ought to have put my money in the bank, and on my arrival I would have received my money back with interest."*) by the *master* in this passage.

The servant never refers to the talent as *money*; but rather maintains that it is *talent*.

And the master only refers to the talent as money, *after* the "*then*" or conditionally, and this is only pertinent *if* the servant's characterizations, ("*you knew that I reap where I did not sow and gather where I scattered no seed*"), of the master were in fact true.

But when the master then speaks to someone else regarding the servant; and is no longer speaking with the condition of the "if" hypothetically having been met; he *then* refers to it as *talent*, ("*take away the talent from him*"); and not money.

It is as though the usage of the term "money" is strictly reserved for use by others only, and used only by what the speaker, (the "master"), believes would be suitable from the servant's perspective—even though that term is never once used by the servant.

The actual word translated here and also in Matthew 25:18 translated as "money" is:

> "694 arguriŏn; neut. Of a presumed der. of 696; *silvery*, i.e. (by impl.) *cash*; spec. a *silverling* (i.e. *drachma* or *shekel*): - money, (piece of) silver (piece)."[30]

And with respect to *arguriŏn* being derived from 696, the same is:

> "696 argurŏs; from argŏs (*shining*); *silver* (the metal, in the articles or coin): - silver."[31]

Donald Trump Candidacy According to Matthew?

This sounds somewhat reasonable, in that *money* would be a fair translation of *arguriŏn* meaning silvery, from *argurŏs*, which is from *argŏs*; given what was purportedly in use back in "those days."

However; note the qualification by Strong that the derivation of *arguriŏn* from 696 is merely *"presumed."*

There is also another problem developing here. This citation contains these two things: Firstly that 696 *argurŏs* is derived from *argŏs*; and then the definition is provided.

However it is the definition of *arg<u>ur</u>ŏs* and not argŏs which is provided as: *"silver* (the metal, in the articles or coin): - silver."

When comparing *arguriŏn*, *argurŏs*, and *argŏs*; there seems to be either additional or missing letters, (ur), depending upon one's perspective; which seems to be a source of confusion.

According to Strong, the word from which *argurŏs* is derived (*argŏs*), is:

> "*692* argŏs; from *1* (as a neg. particle) [*1* is A as used in negation whatever follows and *2041*; *inactive*, i.e. *unemployed*; (by impl.) *lazy, useless*: - barren, idle, slow."[32]

And the above referenced 2041 is:

> "*2041* ĕrgŏn; from a prim. (but obsol.) ĕrgō (to work); toil (as an effort or occupation...."[33]

If this word *ĕrgŏn* sounds familiar, it is

because *ěrgŏn* was the word from which *ěrgazŏmai*; previously *erroneously* translated as "traded," was derived; but that actually means *work*.

Here however, with the addition of the negation; *argŏs* represents its opposite: "'inactive,' or no-work, or the opposite of work."

Thus it seems most reasonable that the original word used in the text, *argŏs*; is a combination of "a" as a prefix, providing "the negation of" whatever follows this prefix; which in this case is that same root of 2041 *ěrgŏn,* which is *ěrgō.*

Thus it seems quite likely that originally the word *argŏs* was aěrgō, (the negation of "a" with ěrgō, as the root of ěrgŏn); and then over time *aěrgō* became *argŏs*.

Based upon this; then describing the talent of the servant with one talent as "*money,*" is quite erroneous. *Laziness* would be the best definition. This is further supported by the fact that the master did in fact refer to this servant as both "wicked" and "lazy," prior to the second appearance of the word translated as "money."

This is merely speculation, but since Argentum, (symbol Ag), is the correct term for the metal commonly known as silver, the roots of this term may in fact be related to a term based upon the concept of a "lazy man's" metal, as silver historically has been about one twentieth the value of gold.

Proverbs 14:23 did tell us that "*in all labor there is profit.*" Thus if there is labor, there must be profit, and a relationship is established between labor and profit. So if there is any labor, then there must be some profit as "all," is "all" inclusive.

Donald Trump Candidacy According to Matthew?

But this is a one way street, in that it does not *preclude* profit without labor. But according to the second half of 14:24, if one assumes that *"mere talk"* is equal to no labor, then poverty and only poverty is where this leads..."] (End of Excerpt)

[The remainder of the analysis of the "Talent Man" parable will be available upon publication of the upcoming new book.]

The following is provided from the most non-political standpoint possible. No endorsement (or non-endorsement) of any candidate or political ideology is either expressed or implied...

It seems that Donald J. Trump has been considering; (some would say threatening); to run for president of the United States for some time. It seems that this desire had been building in him for years, and he finally decided to do something about it.

This is often how a talantŏn will work—assuming of course that it is a talantŏn. The great science fiction writer Robert A. Heinlein was once asked about why he enjoyed writing. Although his exact response is unavailable, he essentially answered: "Good God, what ever gave you the idea I enjoyed writing?" He was then asked why he did it, if he didn't enjoy it. His answer was that he did it because it: "Hurts less to write than to not write."

Later in the chapter containing the above excerpt,

the subject of the "a-talantŏn" is addressed. An a-talantŏn is not of God, but rather is a device of the enemy. The purpose of both the talantŏn and the a-talantŏn is not to get the *tsaba* or H. Sapiens to act, but rather to *choose* to act. An a-talantŏn is a *counterfeit* version of the talantŏn.

However; unlike the a-talantŏn; with the talantŏn, there can be no violations of God's rules. No violations of any of the Commandments are required. This is not to say that one who is "working" a talantŏn will not in the process violate said rules or Commandments; but rather that this is not *required*. Any such violations are *errors* committed by the active party. These in fact represent *deviations* from what actions it is that are required by the talantŏn for success and balance.

With the a-talantŏn, the reverse is true. This is a key in making the determination as to which type of "weight;" (talantŏn vs. a-talantŏn); it is that one is experiencing. If any action inconsistent with the word of God is required in order to satisfy that which seems to be "heavy on one's heart;" then whatever it might otherwise be; is not a talantŏn.

The other main difference is the presence of dunamis, or supernatural power. With an a-talantŏn, the possibility of any significant levels of dunamis is essentially zero.

As previously stated, dunamis is supernatural power, and not natural power. This can manifest in many different forms, and often is not recognized as such until much later.

There are two keys to recognizing dunamis, as opposed to mere natural power:

Donald Trump Candidacy According to Matthew?

Firstly; there must be violations of what is considered to be natural law. The "considered to be" part of course is crucial. Dunamis is not always as immediately obvious as feeding all the people at a picnic with one loaf of bread and a fish. When any cause definitively produces an effect other than that which is definitively "natural," dunamis is likely present. This can manifest in the physical, such as turning water into wine; or can also take place in the non-physical.

Secondly; dunamis or dunamic "acts" generally tend to happen quickly. The miracle that is considered to be the longest in duration; is the provision of manna—which roughly translates as "what is it?" But in actuality this was an act of dunamis provided each day, and not one act lasting years; as manna would not keep. "Happen quickly" can also mean seeming to "come out of nowhere." Perhaps "suddenly" is a better description; i.e. quickly and not expected. However a "dunamisless" a-talantŏn can also seem to happen quickly. The seemingly instant rise of Elvis Presley representing the former; with the rise of ISIS representing the latter.

When a talantŏn is present, this talantŏn is the source of that "heavy on my heart" feeling that tends to prompt one into action. Depending on the nature of the recipient, they: "aint gonna have no peace," until they begin acting or introducing "ergs" into the system.

When natural force is applied, (ergs), in an attempt to balance or remove the weight, the result is that dunamis or supernatural force begins to manifest. Once this begins, seemingly impossible events begin to be observed. Again, this assumes it is in fact a talantŏn that is being "worked." The use of "true talantŏn" is purposely avoided here, as it is arguably tautological. This would be similar to: "his own autobiography;" as to who else could possibly be expected to write his autobiography.

In the "Talent Man" story, the servants had supernatural power (dunamis). They were given weight (talantŏn) according to the amount of dunamis. Two of the servants "worked" this weight by putting energy into the system.

The result of their efforts ("*You were faithful with a few things*"); was additional weight or talantŏns being given to them; and they were put "*in charge of many things; enter into the joy of your master.*" This was done by first giving them additional weight, (talantŏns); and then given, (put in charge of), additional dunamis.

The "*enter into the joy of your master*" part should not be overlooked.

This parable provides an explanation of mechanisms and rules of, (for it is just like); the immaterial realm or the "kingdom of heaven." The "*joy of your master*" part refers to God as the master: "*Well done, good and faithful slave.*"—remembering here that the correct translation is *servant*.

This talantŏn/dunamis/talantŏn process is just that. It is a process, and not designed to be a "one shot deal." However; assuming the process is understood, (which is and was the true purpose of the parable); it nevertheless remains the choice of the recipient as to how far the process proceeds—hence the inclusion of the "one talent man."

It seems fair to say that Donald Trump's entire professional career consisted of a series of processes that were at least *similar* to the above process. He began by borrowing one million dollars from his father; which is and was a lot of money; but not as much as it may seem given the real estate values in Manhattan, even at that time.

Why did he borrow it? In order to "work" a "desire" to build. He put ergs into this desire and began building an empire.

For "some reason" he elected to invest in Manhattan, despite his father's belief that Donald should invest in Brooklyn, as he himself had done. And as of this writing, Donald has grown his assets to somewhere in the ten billion dollar range.

Whether this was completely, partially, or not in any way due to dunamic forces cannot be stated at this juncture.

Whether this was merely a talantŏn/*dynamikós*/talantŏn (natural power) process, or an actual talantŏn/*dunamis*/talantŏn (supernatural power) process requires a bit of study.

What *can* be stated however; is that the level of his personal business success was a highly unusual outcome. This is not to say that it is or was a unique outcome, but clearly a highly unusual outcome. However; assuming that it in fact was this talantŏn/*dunamis* process, and not mere *dynamikós*; it must remembered that the same is available to all. Like many things, it is not the *presence* of the talantŏn that determines success, but rather one's *reaction* to it— once again, as per the generally misunderstood Talent Men parable.

Nevertheless, his personal businesses processes are quite similar to the processes described in the parable. Initially, he was in charge of the "few." He was "good and faithful" with what he was given, and was put in charge of the "many." This being an ongoing lifelong process and not a one time event, as the concepts of "few" and "many" are in fact relative terms. Last year's "many" can become this year's "few."

Does this mean that he never made mistakes? Of course not, because as the old saying goes: "Different levels, different devils." Only "One" was ever able to completely resist the actions of the enemy, and that "One" is not Donald Trump. And the "return" for the enemy is much greater with someone who is successful and well known—hence it is worth the expenditure of much more effort on the part of the enemy.

Donald Trump Candidacy According to Matthew?

It is interesting to compare the common understanding of the characteristics of Donald Trump, with the actualities:

Most would consider the name Donald Trump to be synonymous with champagne and "pheasant under glass;" or perhaps "black tie" galas with priceless cognac. The fact is that he has never consumed an alcoholic beverage in his entire life. He prefers cheeseburgers, and often sends his butler out for one. Why does he send his butler out instead of getting the cheeseburger himself? Likely this is merely an issue of the value of his time, and his personal safety. One might also consider that the gold plated fixtures in his home and airplane could be merely because of the image he believes *should* project, given the nature of his businesses. On the other hand, gold will not rust.

Two things should be asked:

Firstly; How many people have shown more lifelong successes with the talantŏn/*dunamis*/talantŏn process than Donald Trump; even if one is unsure as to whether it is dunamis or dynamikós that was involved? Or more broadly; how many have shown a better understanding of the *process* revealed in the "Talent Man" parable—irrespective of whether the parable was understood, or even known?

And secondly; how many things on the earth represent a greater "many" than the presidency of the United States?

Many would say that Donald Trump actually began his presidential bid back in 1987. As years went on, he became more and more interested in "running," which culminated in his formal decision to do so in June of 2015. This is a rather long term talantŏn; but a talantŏn can sometimes be like that. It must also again be noted, the US Presidency is also a rather large "many"

No matter which aspect of his candidacy is examined; he seems to have broken, and continues to break essentially all of the known rules of politics.

When Trump announced his intentions to run for president, many of the "experts" simply laughed. As the result of being so certain that this "carnival barker" (the words of others), was merely seeking yet more publicity, his "intentions" were simply and summarily dismissed by the "experts."

Early on, Karl Rove was asked about the Trump candidacy and Rove's response was "Ignore him." Ed Rollins commented early on that Trump was "not a viable candidate."

There was; (and still is by many); all of the talk about Trump "having a high floor and a low ceiling." Then as time went on, like an elevator in one of his high rise buildings; both the floor and the ceiling kept rising. Then he became the frontrunner.

Initially, and as the campaign progressed, Trump began making statements that the "experts" were certain would completely sink his campaign; but instead his popularity increased. Often these "controversial" statements were subsequently expropriated by his competitors.

Donald Trump Candidacy According to Matthew?

These "experts'" opinions should be analyzed from a cause-effect perspective. Whatever it was that Trump was saying at any given time; which made these experts certain that Trump would be harmed; represented a cause-effect relationship in their minds. The "rules" of politics dictate that the *effect* of these statements should be a *decrease* in popularity. This rule is based upon many years of experience, hence the term "experts; and thus in a sense represents "natural law." But with Trump, the effect of these statements was exactly the opposite of what would be expected to happen. Thus these many actions of Trump clearly and consistently violated "natural law;" at least in the mind of these "experts."

It must be noted that God will; up to a point; often overlook many of our faults, in order to get something accomplished. He knows that if He required perfection from any of His hosts before utilization by Him; nothing will ever happen. He thus utilizes "what is" rather than what "should be." Although we were created in His "image and likeness," none; (except One); remained or remains so.

In this sense and for good reason, the public is like God. Unlike the "experts;" the public will overlook certain faults in order to get behind someone who seems to be able to get things done.

The experts had the actuality; (that which *is*); and subsequent reality; (that which is *perceived*) completely wrong. The experts perceived; (their reality), only that part of the Trump actuality that consisted of what they considered to be errors on Trump's part. Thus in their minds that was all that mattered, and in their view

Trump should have sunk. Thus; based upon their experience, whatever else represented the actuality of Donald Trump was largely irrelevant.

But the public saw it differently. The public perceived the actuality of Trump as that which the experts (the builders) rejected; and largely rejected that which the experts accepted. To them, any misstatements; (if they in fact were misstatements); on Trumps part, represented only a small part of the Trump actuality.

Trump is perceived by many as a "regular" guy, despite the billions he has amassed. The personal *reality* of the *actuality* of money can vary greatly. Money can be a source of pride, or merely a means of assessing the level of success. If the latter, then all of the usual "trappings" associated with such wealth simply do not matter. It must me remembered that the Bible tell us that it is the *love* of money, and not the money itself that is the root of evil. The Bible does not tell us that the love of *success* is the root of any type of evil. Thus if one's reality of the actuality of money is a measure of success, and it is success that is loved, then there would not be any associated evil.

It is interesting to watch the various players outside the Trump campaign. The so called "establishment" wing of his own party appears to largely hate him. Even those previously considered as outside the "establishment" appear to hate him. Whether or not these are the equivalent to modern day Pharisees or Sadducees, would be a matter of opinion.

There is an Emmanic Principle which states:

Donald Trump Candidacy According to Matthew?

"If you really want to know what a thing
actually is; push on it and see what breaks."

This principle is highly applicable to the so called "establishment" wing of Trump's own political party. In fact; as of this writing, one of the other candidates; (the "establishment" candidate), is continuing to run; even though all admit he has absolutely no mathematical chance of winning the nomination *conventionally*. Yet at the same time he can *only* win the nomination "conventionally." This requires a bit of an explanation.

This other candidate's sole reasons for continuing to run is; to either try and stop Trump from gaining sufficient delegates to win the nomination fairly; and/or to have himself or someone; *anyone*; other than Trump be "anointed" by the party. He is thereby attempting to deliberately thwart the will of the primary voters, by attempting to have the *party* pick the nominee instead—*at the convention*. Said actions are the antithesis of the very democratic process itself. It seems that when the stress of the campaign was placed upon this particular individual; i.e.; via the aforementioned "push;" then his true nature was revealed.

Another candidate is engaging in the proliferation of an "a truth" campaign. Stating "a truth" instead of "the truth" can be one of the three ways of lying: (1) Telling an outright lie; (2) Stating the truth but only part of it; (3) Telling the complete truth, but in such a disbelieving manner that the listener believes the opposite. Claiming to be a devout "Christian," he nevertheless seems to find it necessary to do these things in order to stop Trump. Once again; "push" on it and see what breaks.

This same fellow also has almost no chance winning *conventionally*, (first definition); so in order to be the nominee, he must win it *conventionally*, (second definition). Without commenting on the *quality* of his political views; it can be stated that his views deviate far from the "establishment's" political views. Thus; any belief that he would or even could be chosen by the "establishment," seems to be quite delusional.

One reason for this; is that once the "mere superfluities" of the "purportation" of things such as democracy and the Constitution are stripped away; the "establishment" wings of the Democratic and Republican parties are quite similar. When pushed, it is either the acquisition or the retention of power that is the main driving force for both parties.

Principles such as the public *choosing* their own leader; instead of the same being *appointed* by those who are "anointed," and thus "much wiser" than the public; simply become obstacles to power. These "obstacles" must then be overcome in any way possible that does not include a term in prison.

It matters little that the "establishment" wing of one party openly espouses views which are less antithetical to personal freedom than the other party. The fact is that when either thing or any thing is "pushed;" the truth is revealed.

The present "establishment" Republican's view, is that the people are simply too incompetent to choose their own candidate; and in their view, Donald Trump

Donald Trump Candidacy According to Matthew?

being the consistent frontrunner represents conclusive evidence of this fact. Therefore the "establishment" must step in and thwart the will of the voters. This is: "forgive them for they know not what they do," without the "forgive them for" part.

This is all mentioned here; because it is important to understand that once action is taken (ergs) upon a talantŏn, the enemy immediately takes notice. In fact, the amount of ergs by those who are opposing a person who is "working" a talantŏn, can often be a good "barometer" of the amount of success the person working the talantŏn is actually achieving.

This is particularly interesting to watch; when those who are reputed to be of high moral character engage in actions antithetical to said reputation. Or; when those whose previous views of personal freedom and personal choice (live free or die), suddenly disappear when it comes to the public choosing the party nominee.

Going against one who is "working" a talantŏn, generally requires a large amount of force from the enemy; which he/it would not need to bother with had the talantŏn instead been buried. The amount of force the enemy exerts, is what he/it believes is necessary to counteract the ergs being applied to the talantŏn; and thus can be used to indicate the likelihood of success by the "working" of the talantŏn—at least in the mind of the enemy. But the enemy is incapable of victory against the dunamis created by the application of ergs to a talantŏn. In order to be victorious, the enemy can only be *given* victory; and only by the person with the talantŏn.

Can someone "working" a talantŏn fail? Most certainly; which is precisely how victory is *given* to an enemy who has insufficient power to *claim* it.

These actions of others who are the targets or recipients of these indirect (indirect with respect to Trump) attacks of the enemy are especially noteworthy, with the "reporting" of "what Trump said." This can easily be verified by watching the unedited clips.

For example:

> When Trump is speaking about the Mexican government sending; "They're sending;" criminals into the United States; (just as Fidel Castro once did); with the subject of his comments being the Mexican government; it is reported that Trump hates Hispanics and calls them all criminals. There is also a constant conflating of *legal* and *illegal* immigrants, to make it appear that Trump "hates" all immigrants.

> When Trump comments (appropriately or otherwise) about an individual who just happens to not have a "y chromosome;" (i.e.; a female); it is reported that Trump hates women; as though he is attacking all women, simply because the person he "attacked" happened to be female. Yet the same argument is never raised when he "attacks" men. He is never accused of being "anti-male" because he "attacks" a person who just happens to have said "y

chromosome." And then it is always Trump, and never the "reporter" who is called the sexist. If this "logic" were applied by the reporter on a *non-sexist* basis, the only possible conclusion would be that Trump must then in fact simply hate everyone.

When Trump states that "all lives matter," he is then called a "racist" because he will not make any differentiation as to whether or not a life matters based upon skin color.

These are not mentioned in order to advocate for Trump. Rather; because all of this is merely the result of various levels of weakness on the part of those individuals who are doing much worse than "failing to improve upon the silence." These *deceitful* actions are the direct result of the exploitation of their weaknesses by the one opposing the working of the talantŏn. It must be remembered that "*If it aint truth, it aint God.*"

It should be asked for what possible reason(s) would Donald Trump want the Presidency of the United States?

Some might say money. However; that seems to be a bit short sighted, as there exists somewhere in the neighborhood of ten billion reasons why this is not likely to be so. In addition, he would have to detach himself from his personal interests; and instead settle for the salary provided for the presidency—a salary which he has already said he will not accept. Furthermore; he likely has already lost more money from giving up "The Apprentice," alone, than he could ever recoup legally as a "politician."

Some might say power. Again, it is unclear whether Donald Trump would have more or less power as president, than he currently has. Clearly he has had substantial power over many politicians of both parties, for many years; as a result of his donations to them—something which his opponents dishonestly try to proffer as Trump's support for Democratic *political* positions.

Donald Trump himself stated why it is he wants to be President, but it seems many simply do not believe him.

He said that he loves his country, and indicated that he wants to use whatever he has that made his company great, for the benefit of the country. He further indicated that he simply wants to do for his country, what it is that he did for his company.

Given the enormous amount of time and effort (ergs) by him; and given the fact that Donald Trump has paid for his campaign without taxpayer dollars, or donations from special interests; he should be given the courtesy of being believed with regard to his motivations. Furthermore; we all; even those who may disagree with him; owe him thanks and due respect for what he has thus far undertaken.

Whether or not Donald Trump is "working" a talantŏn, and what the significance of this might be; is for each of us to determine.

ABOUT THE MEEKRAKER SERIES

What on earth is a MeekRaker?
This word can be broken down into two parts "Meek" and "Raker." Capital letters were used in order to minimize any mispronunciations such as Mee-kraker; but the "etymology" is actually the fusion of these two words.

What is meek? And who in their right mind would ever want to be meek? Courage, strength, and bravery are characteristics that are generally considered desirable; but meek? No thanks. Unfortunately, the meaning of this word has been distorted over time to include things such as timidity, or shyness; weakness, or cowardice, but this is not; or rather should not be so.

Chambers states:

> "meek adj. Probably before 1200 meok gentle, humble, in Ancrene Riwle; later mec (probably about 1200, in the *The Ormlum*);

> borrowed from a Scandanavian source (Compare Old Icelandic mjukr soft pliant gentle...."[AT-1]

These origins seem to be adjectival in nature, and describe a condition of humility or softness. Thus a meek person, by these definitions would indicate a humble or soft person. The opposite of this would then be a person who is prideful or hard.

Humble vs. prideful is an easy one. Who would want to be prideful? The Bible is replete with warnings about pride; and it was pride that started all of the messes to begin with. Pride may make one "feel good" for a short period of time, but as previously referenced; the Bible is quite clear that on that path there lies destruction.

But what does the Bible actually have to say about being a meek person?

- It tells us that the meek shall (*not will or might*) inherit the earth.[AT-2]
- It further tells us that the meek will be guided in judgment will be taught His way.[AT-3]
- The meek will be lifted up by the Lord, and He will cast the wicked down to the ground.[AT-4]
- He will save all the meek of the earth.[AT-5]

And what about the Bible's statements regarding being "hard?"

About the MeekRaker Series Title

- "For their heart was hardened."[AT-6] "Have ye your heart yet hardened?"[AT-7]
- "... their eyes and hardened their heart."[AT-8]
- "But they and our fathers dealt proudly, and hardened their necks, and hearkened not to thy commandments, and refused to obey, neither were mindful of thy wonders that thou didst among them; but hardened their necks, and in their rebellion..."[AT-9]
- "Happy is the man that feareth always: But he that hardeneth his heart shall fall into mischief."[AT-10]
- "He that being often reproved hardeneth his neck, shall suddenly be destroyed, and that without remedy."[AT-11]

The actual word in all of these citations which is translated as hard is:

"4456 poroo (a kind of stone); to *petrify*, i.e. (fig.) to *indurate* (*render stupid* or *callous*): - blind, harden.[AT-12]

With respect to hard, there is a clear Scriptural relationship between the same and disobedience; not being "mindful" of God performing wonders in one's life, rebellious, falling into "mischief," and being "destroyed," "without remedy."

In addition, by the very definition of the original word, one who is "hard" is also stupid callous and blind. (If a physical heart were actually to turn into stone, you are just dead; so surely that definition does not apply in this context or usage.)

Thus, meek or soft; that being the opposite of hard; would tend to be obedient, be mindful of God performing wonders, not rebellious, not falling into mischief, and not destroyed. Furthermore, one would not be "stupid," "callous" or "blind."

The use of the term meek as "soft," also implies *teachable*.

Hardhead: will not change mind. Hardhearted: will not change heart. Hard necked: junction between head and heart is hard, and will not permit mental change to be transmitted to change the heart.

If it is firmly established that the term "revelation" has the prerequisite of being *the* truth; when confronted with potential revelation; it has been the authors' experiences that hard persons; specifically those of the head, neck, and heart variety; will generally behave according to the "Three A's:"

> A_1 is *anger*. This is the first response. This anger is not so much because there is a remote chance that they may be wrong, but rather when it is somewhat clear that they *are* wrong. This would be best illustrated as a line on a graph rising from left to right; with the level of anger represented by the vertical axis, and time represented by the horizontal axis.
>
> A_2 is *argument*. This generally begins with emotionally (anger) driven arguments. As

the arguments begin to fail, the level and usually the slope of A_1 will increase. When all possible arguments, logical, relevant or otherwise have been proffered, the original arguments will then return. This would be best illustrated as a circle under the rising anger line referenced above. Often, what is just under the skin, (which is generally the reason for the pride and subsequent anger) will pop its "head" out; revealing things previously unknown about this individual.

A_3 is *absconding*. When all of the arguments and the repetition thereof have unquestionably failed, the hard person will generally abscond; or run away. This may be represented by actual physical separation, changing the subject or in some other manner. This could be perceived as the disappearance of the anger line, but is only subjective; as the true level of anger then becomes somewhat hidden.

Contrarily, the *meek* will weigh the value of any purported revelation; and then decide precisely what it is that merits their belief. Sincere questioning and even some arguments will be presented; but here not with the primary purpose of proving that they, the inquirer, is correct; but rather to understand precisely what it is that this revelation represents; knowing that if it in fact does represent revelation, then this will be to their benefit. A logical decision will then be made with respect to what constitutes the truth.

The primary basis for the actions of a "hard-head," is *emotional*. The primary basis for the actions of the meek; although perhaps including some emotional factors; (i.e. passion); is largely *intellectual*.

In a sense, the purpose of a rake is to separate the soft from the hard. The Bible refers to separating the wheat from the chaff, the silver from the dross; hence the origin of "*MeekRaker*". Meek or hard is not so much determined by what one believes; but rather by the *process* involved in making these determinations.

Bibliography

1) *New American Standard Bible: 1995 update. 1995 (Matthew 25:14-30) The Lockman Foundation: Lahabra, CA*

2) *New American Standard Bible: 1995 update. 1995 (Matthew 25:1) The Lockman Foundation: Lahabra, CA*

3) *Strong, James. Strong's Exhaustive Concordance of the Bible.* © *1890 James Strong, Madison, NJ p. 53 (Greek)*

4) *Strong, James. Strong's Exhaustive Concordance of the Bible.* © *1890 James Strong, Madison, NJ p. 53 (Greek)*

5) *Strong, James. Strong's Exhaustive Concordance of the Bible.* © *1890 James Strong, Madison, NJ p. 474*

6) *Strong, James. Strong's Exhaustive Concordance of the Bible.* © *1890 James Strong, Madison, NJ p. 18 (Greek)*

7) *Strong, James. Strong's Exhaustive Concordance of the Bible.* © *1890 James Strong, Madison, NJ p. 936*

8) *Strong, James. Strong's Exhaustive Concordance of the Bible. © 1890 James Strong, Madison, NJ p. 937*

9) *Strong, James. Strong's Exhaustive Concordance of the Bible. © 1890 James Strong, Madison, NJ p. 24 (Greek)*

10) *Strong, James. Strong's Exhaustive Concordance of the Bible. © 1890 James Strong, Madison, NJ p. 937*

11) *Strong, James. Strongest Strong's Exhaustive Concordance of the Bible. © 2001, Zondervan, Grand Rapids MI p. 1068*

12) *New Open Bible, © 1990, 1985, 1983, Thomas Nelson Inc. p. 31*

13) *Strong, James. Strong's Exhaustive Concordance of the Bible. © 1890 James Strong, Madison, NJ p. 55 (Hebrew)*

14) *Strong, James. Strong's Exhaustive Concordance of the Bible. © 1890 James Strong, Madison, NJ p. 55 (Hebrew)*

15) *Strong, James. Strong's Exhaustive Concordance of the Bible. © 1890 James Strong, Madison, NJ p. 71 (Greek)*

16) *Strong, James. Strong's Exhaustive Concordance of the Bible. © 1890 James Strong, Madison, NJ p. 75 (Greek) "5342 phĕrō; a prim. verb (for which other and appar. not cognate ones are used in certain tenses only); namely,... ĕnĕgkō; to "bear" or carry (in a very wide application, lit. and fig., as follows): - be, bear, bring (forth), carry, come, +*

let her drive, be driven, endure, go on, lay, lead, move, reach, rushing, uphold."

17) *Strong, James. Strong's Exhaustive Concordance of the Bible. © 1890 James Strong, Madison, NJ p. 24 (Greek) "1411 dunamis; from 1410; force (lit. or fig.); spec. miraculous power (usually by impl. a miracle itself); - ability, abundance, meaning, might (-ily, -y, - y deed), (worker of) miracle (-s), power, strength, violence, mighty (wonderful) work." (FN) "1410 dunamai; of uncert. affin.; to be able or possible: - be able, can (do, + - not), could, may, might, be possible, be of power."*

18) *Chambers Dictionary of Etymology. Copyright © 1988 The H. W. Wilson Company, New York, NY p. 308*

19) *New American Standard Bible: 1995 update. 1995 (Proverbs 30:1) The Lockman Foundation: Lahabra, CA*

20) *King James Bible, Proverbs 30:1*

21) *New American Standard Bible: 1995 update. 1995 (Malachi 1:1) The Lockman Foundation: Lahabra, CA*

22) *King James Bible Malachi 1:1*

23) *Strong, James. Strong's Exhaustive Concordance of the Bible. © 1890 James Strong, Madison, NJ p. 73 (Hebrew) "4853 massâ'; from 5375; a burden; spec. tribute, or (abstr.) porterage; fig. an utterance, chiefly a doom, espec. singing; mental, desire: - burden, carry   away, prophesy, x they set, song, tribute."*

24) *Strong, James. Strong's Exhaustive Concordance of the Bible. © 1890 James Strong, Madison, NJ p. 80 (Hebrew) "5375 nâsâ' or nâcâh; a prim. root; to lift in a great variety of applications, lit. and fig. absol. and rel. (as follows): - accept, advance arise, (able to, [armour], suffer to) bear (-er, up) bring (forth), ..."*

25) *New American Standard Bible: 1995 update. 1995 (Luke 12:48) The Lockman Foundation: Lahabra, CA*

26) *Strong, James. Strong's Exhaustive Concordance of the Bible. © 1890 James Strong, Madison, NJ p. 32 (Greek) 2038 ĕrgazŏmai; mid. from 2041; to toil (as a task, occupation, etc.), (by impl.) effect, be engaged in or with, etc.: - commit, do, labor for, minister about, trade (by) work." (FN) "2041 ĕrgŏn; from a prim. (but obsol.) ĕrgō (to work); toil (as an effort or occupation); by impl. and act: - deed, doing, labour, work."*

27) *Strong, James. Strong's Exhaustive Concordance of the Bible. © 1890 James Strong, Madison, NJ p. 32 (Greek)*

28) *New American Standard Bible: 1995 update. 1995 (Proverbs 14:23) The Lockman Foundation: Lahabra, CA*

29) *Strong, James. Strong's Exhaustive Concordance of the Bible. © 1890 James Strong, Madison, NJ p. 38 (Greek)*

30) *Strong, James. Strong's Exhaustive Concordance of the Bible. © 1890 James Strong, Madison, NJ p. 15 (Greek)*

Donald Trump Candidacy According to Matthew?

31) *Strong, James. Strong's Exhaustive Concordance of the Bible. © 1890 James Strong, Madison, NJ p. 15 (Greek)*

32) *Strong, James. Strong's Exhaustive Concordance of the Bible. © 1890 James Strong, Madison, NJ p. 15 (Greek)*

33) *Strong, James. Strong's Exhaustive Concordance of the Bible. © 1890 James Strong, Madison, NJ p. 32 (Greek)*

About the MeekRaker Series Title

AT1 *Chambers Dictionary of Etymology.* Copyright © 1988 The H. W. Wilson Company, New York, NY p.648
AT2 *www.kingjamesbibleonline.org* (KJV) (Matt.5:5) retrieved June 2011
AT3 *www.kingjamesbibleonline.org* (KJV) (Ps. 25:9) retrieved June 2011
AT4 *www.kingjamesbibleonline.org* (KJV) (Ps. 147:6) retrieved June 2011
AT5 *www.kingjamesbibleonline.org* (KJV) (Ps. 76:9) retrieved June 2011
AT6 *www.kingjamesbibleonline.org* (KJV) (Mark 6:52)

retrieved June 2011
AT7 *www.kingjamesbibleonline.org* (KJV) (Mark 8:17) retrieved June 2011
AT8 *www.kingjamesbibleonline.org* (KJV) (John 12:40) retrieved June 2011
AT9 *www.kingjamesbibleonline.org* (KJV) (Neh. 9:16) retrieved June 2011
AT10 *www.kingjamesbibleonline.org* (KJV) (Prov. 28:14) retrieved June 2011
AT11 *www.kingjamesbibleonline.org* (KJV) (Prov. 29:1) retrieved June 2011
AT12 Strong, James. *Strong's Exhaustive Concordance of the Bible.* © 1890 James Strong, Madison, NJ p. 63 (Greek)

Other Fine QPG Publications:

MeekRaker Beginnings...

From the inside flap of *"MeekRaker Beginnings..."*

"The primary purpose of this tome, is the reconciliation of the word of God with science; and to do so in such a manner as to be rendered inarguable by any rational mind. As stated in the Preface: "One must choose between being a "man of science" or a believer," because they are generally considered to be mutually exclusive. If one agrees that words mean things, then an unbiased fair read of God's Word presents no such paradox. But one must read what God actually said, not merely what one thinks He said, what one was told He said, what one wished He said, or would rather He had said."

Wisdom Essentials—*The Pentalogy*

"That Which is Difficult If Not Impossible to Find Anywhere Else—All In One Volume. Vol. I"

But there are many other effects for which no material cause can be found. In *"Donald Trump*

Candidacy According to Matthew?," his meteoric rise and seeming inability to fail are explained according to Biblical principles. Since this is a non-political work, his success was not actually prophesied, but no other conclusion could possibly have been drawn—*and this was published long before he was even nominated.*

In "*SHÂMAR TO SHARIA,*" the process of radical indoctrination is analyzed, and is shown to be a perversion of that very same thing God instructed man to do with the Commandments, and how this is not in any way limited to terrorists.

"*It's Not Just A Theory*" examines the relationship between behavior and longevity according to both science and the Scriptures; and "according to both" also includes major consistencies.

"*Calvary's Hidden Truths*" reveals many unknown facts about what actually occurred at that time.

"*Inevitable Balance*" scientifically and Biblically explains that which is often observed but rarely understood: Why "What Goes Around Comes Around;" AKA *karma*, or the "law of compensation."

STATISTS SAVING ONE

"The Malignant Sophistry of Rights Removal by the Far Left"

"...under the umbrella of "liberals" or "liberalism;" (as used today); there are actually two separate and distinct groups:

"True liberals believe very much in what they promulgate. They are truly concerned with the welfare of citizens, and they believe in policies that will benefit the same—at least in their view. There are neither nefarious purposes, nor any intellectual dishonesty. Their objective is to improve the quality of life (and longevity), for as many people as possible.

"...Conservatives and liberals can often agree on the ends; but vastly disagree on the means. Giving a hungry person a fish is kind; but to conservatives, teaching him how to fish seems to be a better long term solution. It is not that conservatives object to the temporary giving of the fish; but rather they object to not teaching him how to fish.

"True liberals believe in the dignity of man; and promulgate policies in furtherance of this belief.
"Statists; the other group usually and often erroneously grouped under the "liberal" umbrella; are another matter. It is because of agreements with liberal policy that they are usually grouped under this liberal

umbrella; but their motivations, purposes and beliefs are entirely different—arguably antithetical—to true liberalism."

OSTIUM AB INFERNO
[*The Opening From Hell*]

"The Original Monograph - According to the Father, The Christ Son and The Holy Ghost"

"What is hell?
Why is there a hell?
What openings from "hell" exist?
What is the truth about "Abraham's Bosom?" And how does this or do these affect man?
What are angels? Are angels named such because of structure or function? Precisely why were some angels sent to hell? Is it true that one third were banished to hell? And when did this all happen?
Much of that which is fanciful has been written about these questions. But the answers should not be sought from that which is the product of men's imaginations—albeit these may provide interesting reading. Rather; the answers should be sought from, and always remain: "according to The Father, The Christ Son, and The Holy Ghost." (Written in English.)

REINCARNATION —A REASONABLE INQUIRY

"Often times it is emotion(s) and not facts that determine what it is that is believed to be 'in fact so.'"

"When truth and perceived practicality conflict; unfortunately it is truth that often becomes the sacrificial lamb."

"He that answereth a matter before he heareth it, it is folly and shame unto him."
—Proverbs 18:13 (KJV)

On its way—

> QPG Publications are available
> wherever you buy fine books.

www.ingramcontent.com/pod-product-compliance
Lightning Source LLC
Chambersburg PA
CBHW030101100526
44591CB00008B/224